Let's Glue the Pancake in Place

To Parents: This activity helps to build fine motor skills. Cut out the pancake at the bottom right of the page and give it to your child to glue in place. Your child should glue the pancake so that it stays within the boundaries of the plate.

GOOD JOB!

Sticker

Glue the pancake onto the plate. Then, pretend to eat it.

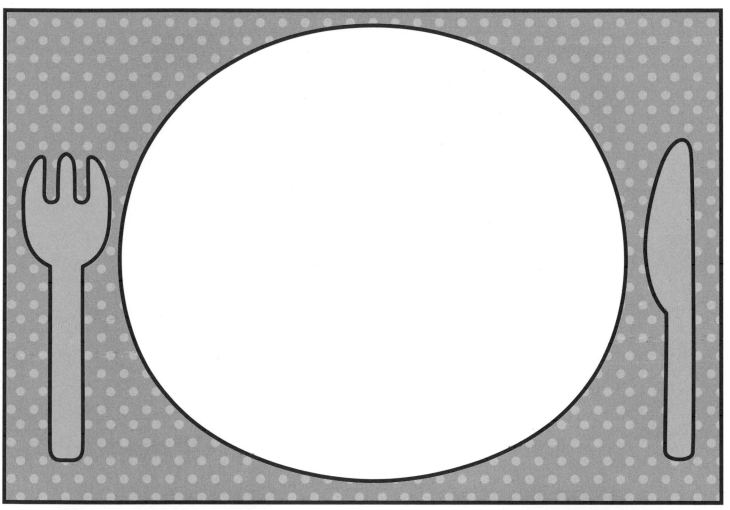

Parents: Cut out the pancake for your child.

Let's Give Panda a Bandage

To Parents: This activity helps develop fine motor skills. While your child is applying the sticker, say, "Let's hope Panda feels better soon."

Sticker

GOOD JOB!
Sticker

Panda cut his forehead and is crying. Let's help Panda feel better.

Place the bandage sticker where Panda is hurt.

Glue

Example

Let's Find the Different Food

To Parents: Here, your child will work on comparing different objects. After your child places the red sticker on or near the object that is different, ask him or her to name the objects in the pictures.

GOOD JOB!

Sticker

One object is different from the others. Find the object and put the ● sticker on it.

Let's Color the Vegetables

To Parents: This activity fosters your child's ability to pick matching colors. Make sure your child chooses the same color as the vegetable.

GOOD JOB!

Sticker

Color each white circle with the matching color for each vegetable.

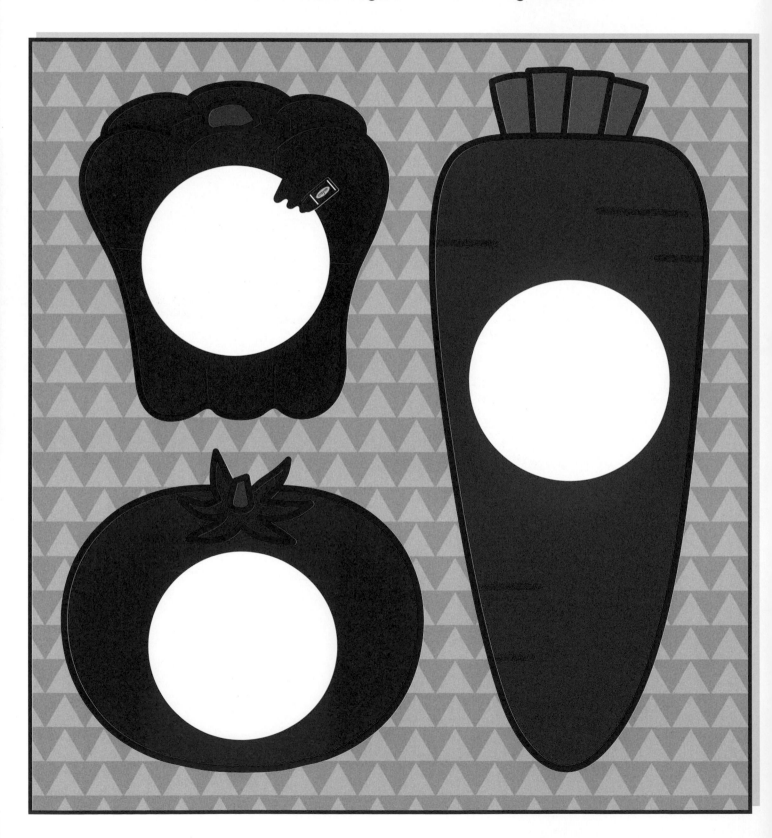

Let's Find the Different Ice Cream

To Parents: In this activity, your child will practice comparing different objects. Ask your child, "Which ice cream cone is different from the rest?"

One object is different from the others. Find the object and put the sticker on it.

Let's Make Dinner

To Parents: This activity focuses on creativity and handwriting. Encourage your child to draw the spaghetti and place the meatball stickers anywhere on the plate.

Draw spaghetti on the plate. Then, put meatball stickers on top.

Let's Play Peekaboo

To Parents: This activity focuses on your child's ability to express himself or herself. When you open the folded paper, say, "Peekaboo!"

Play peekaboo by opening and closing the folded paper.

How to Play

First, fold the paper. Then, open it up.

Fold up

Parents: Cut this line for your child.

Let's Color the Balloons

To Parents: In this activity, your child will practice picking the matching color. Ask your child which color he or she likes best.

Color each white circle with the matching color for each balloon.

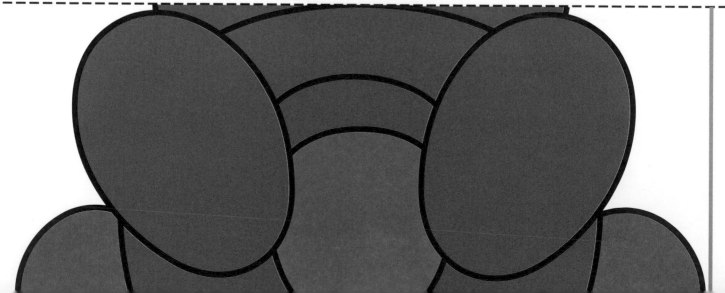

Let's Do Origami

To Parents: Origami is the Japanese art of paper folding. Folding paper builds fine motor skills and develops a child's ability to focus. After your child folds the bus and the dog, save them to be used on page 11.

Fold the bus and the dog. Use them in the activity on page 11.

How to Make It

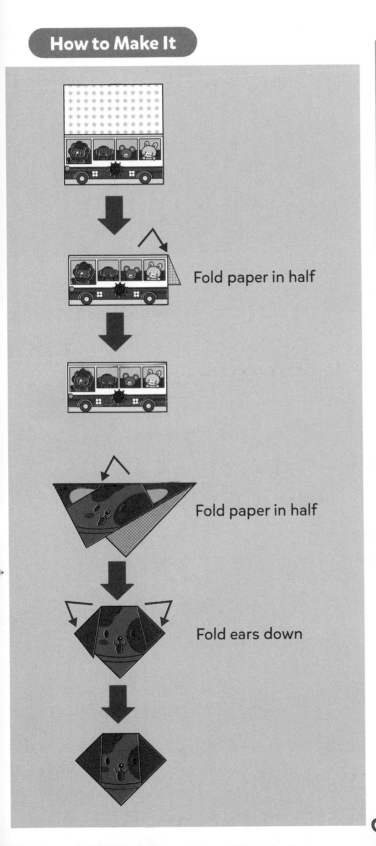

Fold paper in half

Fold paper in half

Fold ears down

Parents: Cut out the bus and dog for your child.

Fold down

Fold up

Fold down

Fold up

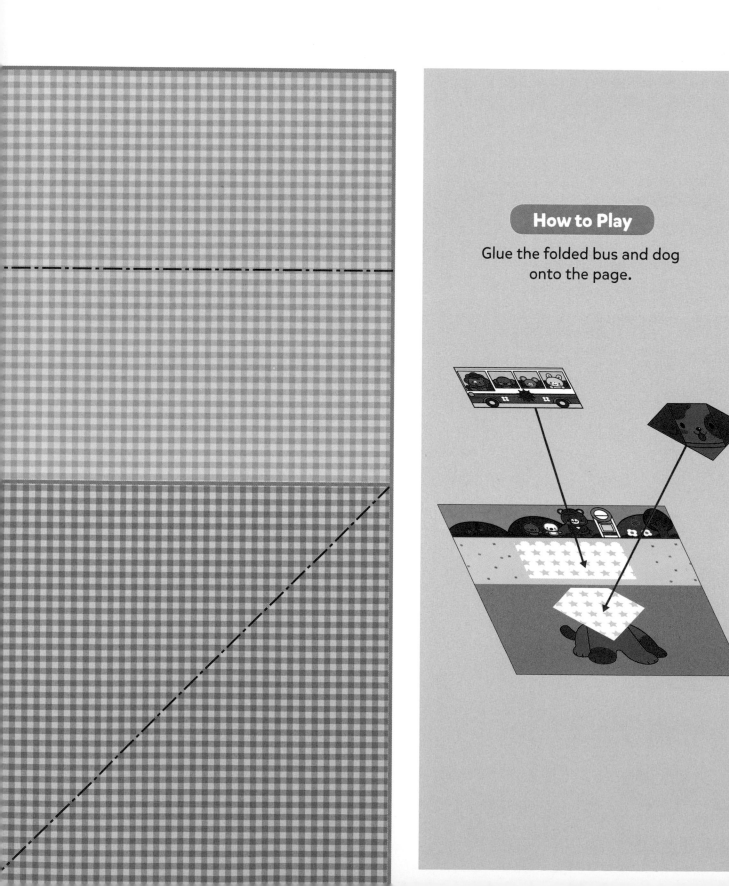

How to Play

Glue the folded bus and dog
onto the page.

Let's Complete the Picture

To Parents: To help your child decide where the bus and dog should go, ask, "Where does the dog go?" and "Where does the bus go?" Then, ask your child how he or she knew where to put each item.

Glue the bus and dog where they belong in the picture.

Glue

Glue

Glue

Let's Find the Animal Tails

To Parents: Here, your child will practice looking at parts and determining what the whole looks like. Help your child name the animals if he or she does not know them.

Look at the picture in each ⭕. Find the animal that has each tail. Point to the tail, and then point to its matching animal. Say the name of the animal out loud.

Let's Find Out Which Is Bigger

To Parents: This activity fosters an understanding of size difference. Point to the dog and ask your child to tell you what it is. Then, point to the cow and do the same.

Sticker

There is a cow and a dog in the picture. Which one is bigger?

Put the  sticker on the bigger animal.

Let's Make a Banana

To Parents: First, cut out the yellow rectangle and give it to your child. Encourage your child to make the banana shape he or she likes and not just copy the example. Tearing and gluing help build fine motor skills.

Tear the yellow paper into the shape of a banana.

Then, glue the banana inside the basket.

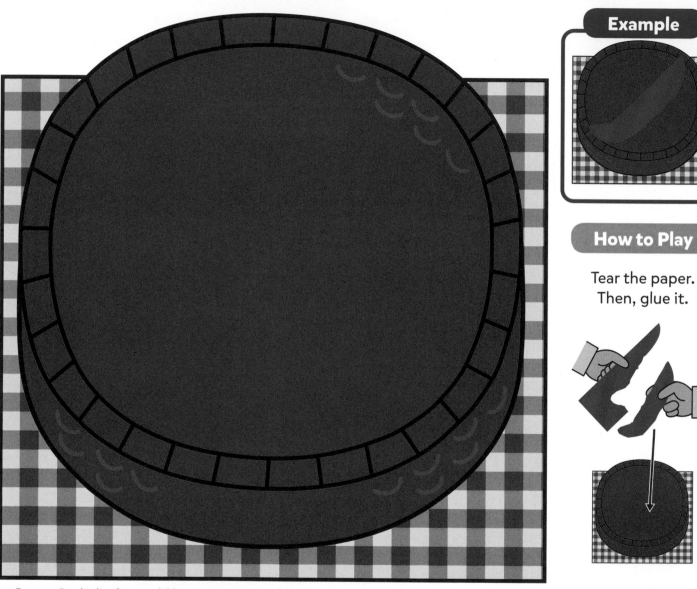

Example

How to Play

Tear the paper.
Then, glue it.

Parents: Cut this line for your child.

Let's Make Strawberries

To Parents: Cut out the red rectangle and give it to your child to tear into several strawberries.

Tear the red paper into the shape of strawberries.

Then, glue the strawberries onto the cake.

Example

Parents: Cut this line for your child.

Let's Draw Lines

To Parents: Here, your child will practice the line-drawing skills needed for proper handwriting. Guide your child to follow the gray dotted line with his or her finger. Then, have your child trace the line with a crayon.

Trace the lines from ➡ to ➡.

Make sounds like a car or a bus as you trace each line.

Let's Make Animals

To Parents: This activity focuses on your child's ability to express himself or herself. Guide your child to make animal movements with his or her hand and fingers. Make sounds like the swooshing of the elephant's trunk and the snapping of the alligator's jaws.

Sticker

Put stickers on your hand to turn it into an elephant.

Then, put stickers on your hand to turn it into an alligator.

Swish, swish goes the elephant's trunk.

Move your finger to make it look like an elephant's trunk.

ELEPHANT

The alligator's mouth goes:

Snap!

Open and close your hand to make it look like a hungry alligator's mouth.

ALLIGATOR

Let's Draw Lines

To Parents: Line-drawing skills like these are needed for proper handwriting. Guide your child to follow the gray dotted line with his or her finger. Then, have your child trace the line with a crayon.

The eggs just hatched, and the chicks were born.

Trace the lines from ➡ to ➡. Say "cheep cheep" while you trace each line.

Let's Find the Matching Cakes

To Parents: This activity focuses on your child's observational skills. Ask your child to point to the cakes that are the same, and then draw a line between each of the three pairs.

Draw a line to connect each cake with its match.

Let's Name the Objects

To Parents: This activity encourages healthy habits. Help your child name objects he or she sees every day to naturally broaden vocabulary and foster better communication. During your next bath time, ask your child to name the objects around the room.

Sticker

Find the washcloth and the water.

When you find them, put the sticker on them.

Let's Color the Animals

To Parents: In this activity, your child will practice identifying and matching colors. Help your child name the animals if he or she does not know them.

Color each white circle with the matching color for each sea creature.

Let's Be Ants

To Parents: This activity focuses on your child's ability to express himself or herself. Point to the ants in the picture. Say, "The ants are tiny and have antennae on their heads. Let's be ants." Crouch down and move your fingers around like an ant would move its antennae.

GOOD JOB!

Sticker

Pretend to be tiny ants and walk around.

Let's Find the Animal Faces

To Parents: In this activity, your child will practice matching objects with names. Cut out the animal faces below. After your child glues the faces in place, ask, "Where is the pig's mouth?" and "Where are the raccoon's eyes?" Encourage your child to point out the ears and noses too.

Glue the faces and onto the pictures.

Parents: Cut out the faces for your child.

Let's Color the Eggs

To Parents: Show your child the example picture if he or she needs help deciding what color the yolks should be. Explain that these eggs are called sunny side-up eggs.

Color the yolks in the eggs.

Example

Glue

Glue

Let's Brush Hippo's Teeth

To Parents: This activity is designed to build fine motor skills while developing healthy habits. Guide your child to fold the toothbrush along the dotted line, and then brush Hippo's teeth with an up-and-down motion.

GOOD JOB!
Sticker

Fold the toothbrush. Then, brush Hippo's teeth.

Parents: Cut out the toothbrush for your child.

How to Play

Fold in half.

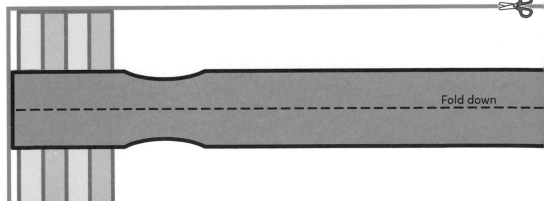

Fold down

Brush Hippo's teeth.

Let's Color the Fruit

To Parents: Ask your child to name the color of each fruit and to choose the appropriate crayon to use. Then, ask your child to name each fruit. This activity helps your child learn to recognize colors.

Color each white circle with the matching color for the fruit.

Let's Draw Straight Lines

To Parents: In this activity, your child will practice line-drawing skills, which are needed for proper handwriting. Guide your child to follow the gray dotted line with his or her finger. Then, have your child trace the line with a crayon.

Trace the line from ➡ to ➡. Make rain sounds as you trace each line.

Let's Draw Curved Lines

To Parents: This activity is designed to teach how to draw curved lines for handwriting practice. Have your child follow each gray dotted line with his or her finger and then with a crayon.

GOOD JOB!

Sticker

Show how the insects fly away from the flowers. Follow the lines from ➡ to ➡.

Then, trace the lines with a crayon.

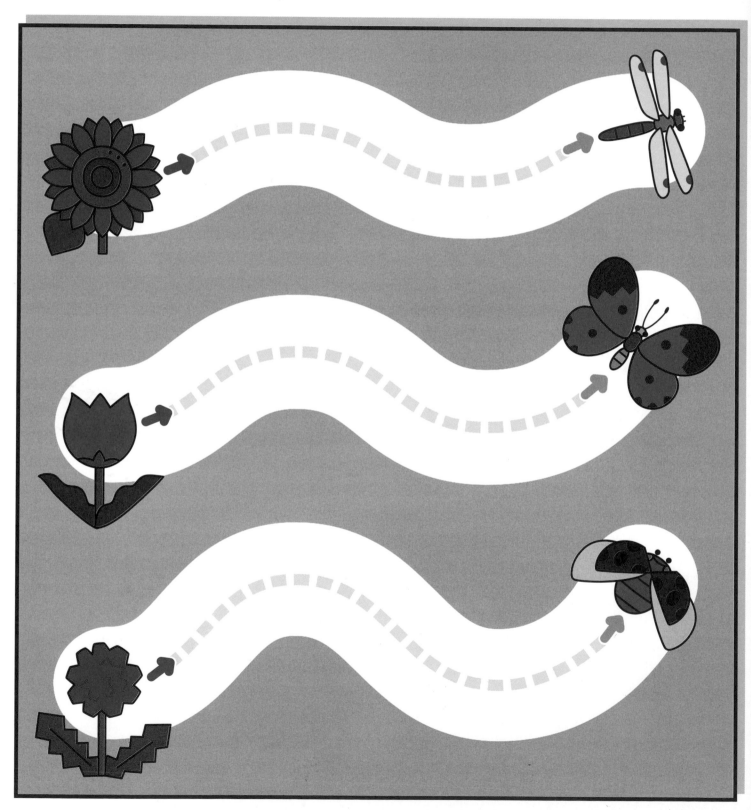

Let's Practice Manners

To Parents: This activity is designed to build healthy habits and communication skills. After putting Rabbit to bed, ask your child what she or he might say just after getting up in the morning.

What do you say before you go to sleep?

Place the blanket over Rabbit, and say it out loud.

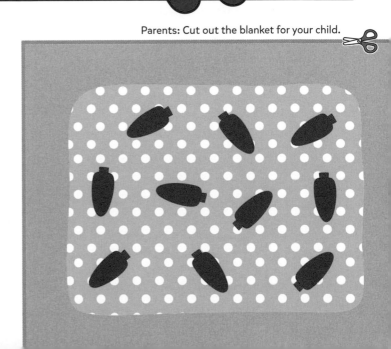

Parents: Cut out the blanket for your child.

How to Play

Good night

Place the blanket over Rabbit, and say, "Good night."

Let's Find the Longer Train

To Parents: Be sure your child looks at the length of the train, not the number of train cars in each train.

 Sticker

 GOOD JOB! Sticker

Which of the two trains is longer? Put the ⬤ sticker on the longer train.

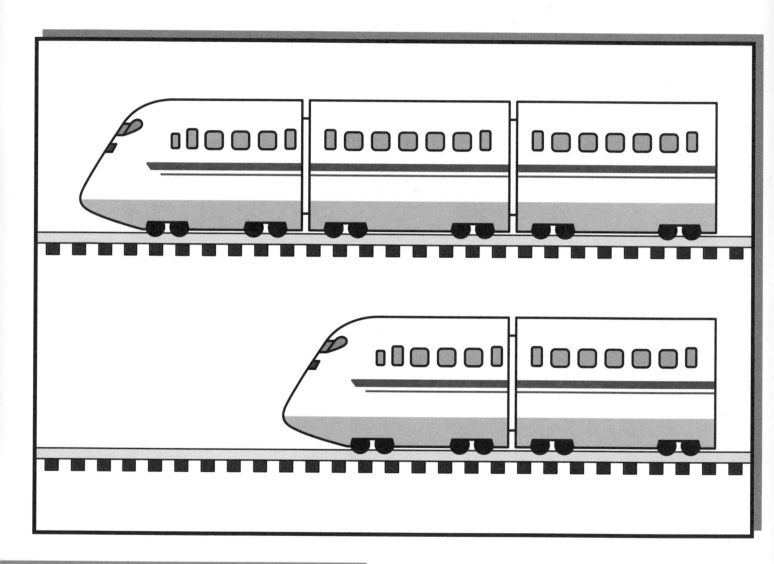

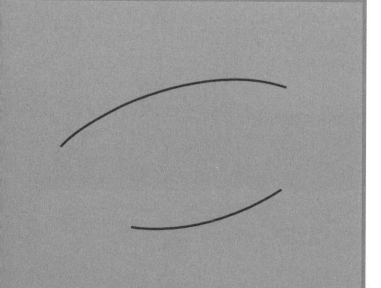

Let's Trace the Letter

To Parents: Here, your child will practice handwriting and work on language skills too. After your child traces the letter, say, "*A* is for *apple.*" Have your child trace the gray dotted line with a crayon if he or she is able.

Name the fruit in the picture. Say it out loud.

Then, trace the line from ➡ to ➡ with your finger.

APPLES

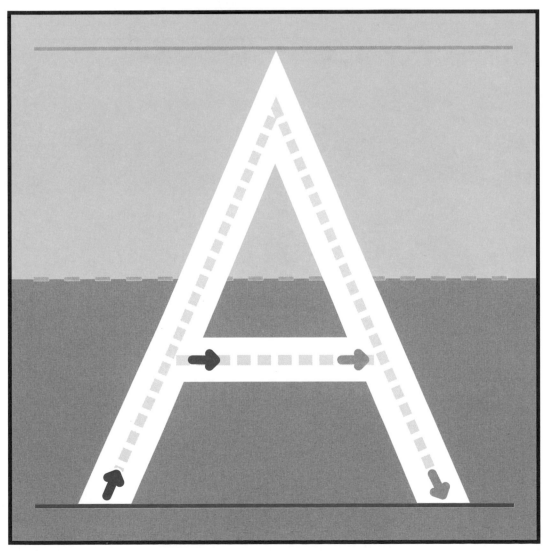

A

Let's Trace the Letter

To Parents: This activity fosters proper handwriting and language development. Have your child trace the gray dotted line with a crayon if he or she is ready.

Name the animals in the picture. Say it out loud.

Then, trace the line from ➡ to ➡ with your finger.

BEARS

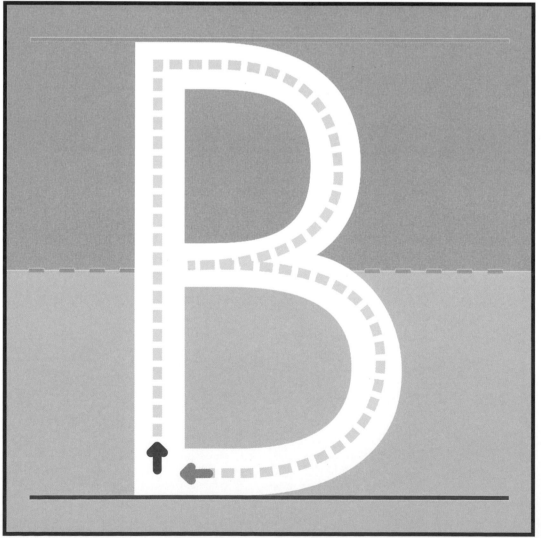

B

Let's Play Card Games

To Parents: Cut out the cards from pages 33 to 38 to make twelve game cards.

Put the four cards in a pile. We will play a game with them soon!

Parents: Cut out the cards for your child.

SOCKS

HAT

UNDERWEAR

SHOES

UMBRELLA

PANTS

PAJAMAS

MITTENS

Let's Play Card Games

To Parents: Cut out the cards from pages 33 to 38 to make twelve game cards.

Add these cards to the pile. We will play a game with them soon!

LION

PANDA

ELEPHANT

DOLPHIN

PENGUIN

SQUIRREL

CAT

DOG

GOOD JOB!
Sticker

Let's Play Card Games

To Parents: Cut out the cards from pages 33 to 38 to make twelve game cards.

Add these cards to the pile. We will play a game with them soon!

Parents: Cut out the cards for your child.

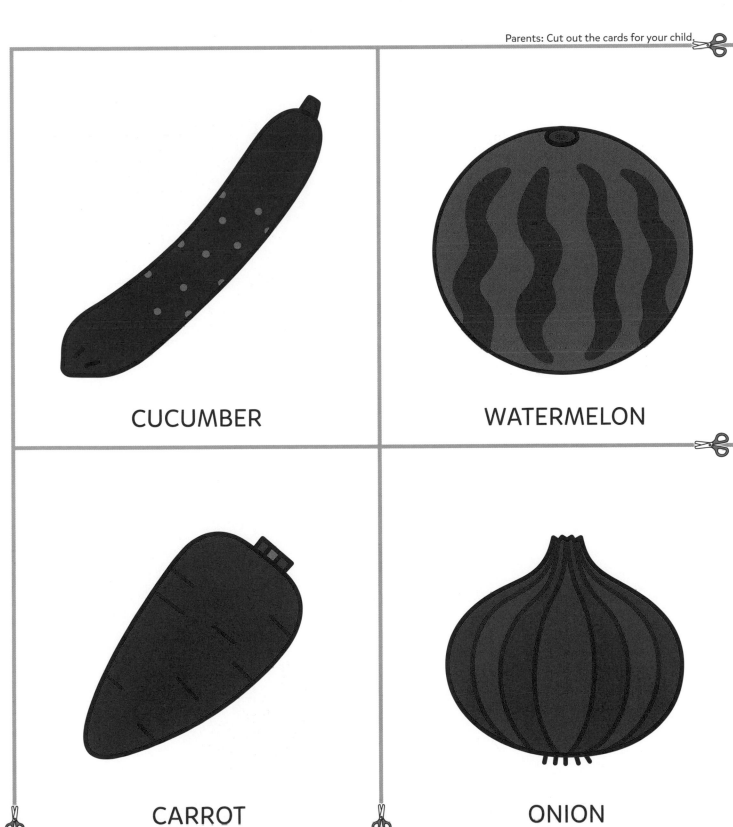

CUCUMBER

WATERMELON

CARROT

ONION

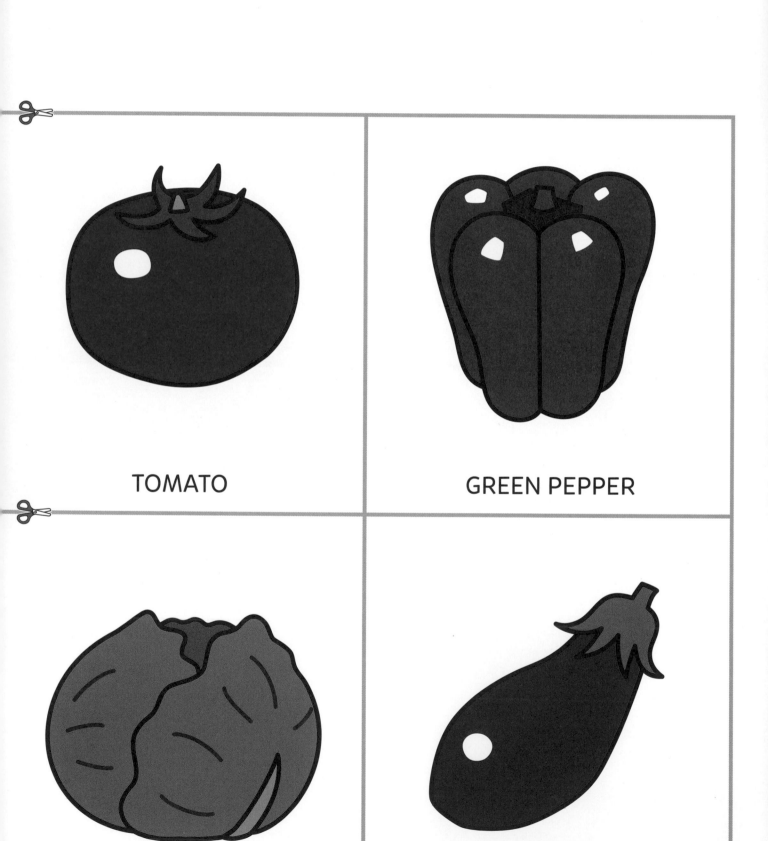

TOMATO

GREEN PEPPER

LETTUCE

EGGPLANT

Let's Play Card Games

To Parents: Cut out the case below. Help your child make the folds and place the stickers. Directions for how to play the card games are on page 40.

Sticker

Fold this case for your cards. Then, start playing the card games!

Parents: Cut out the case for your child.

How to Make the Case

First, fold the case in half here.

Second, fold here.

Third, fold here.

Flip it over.

Apply the stickers to hold the case together.

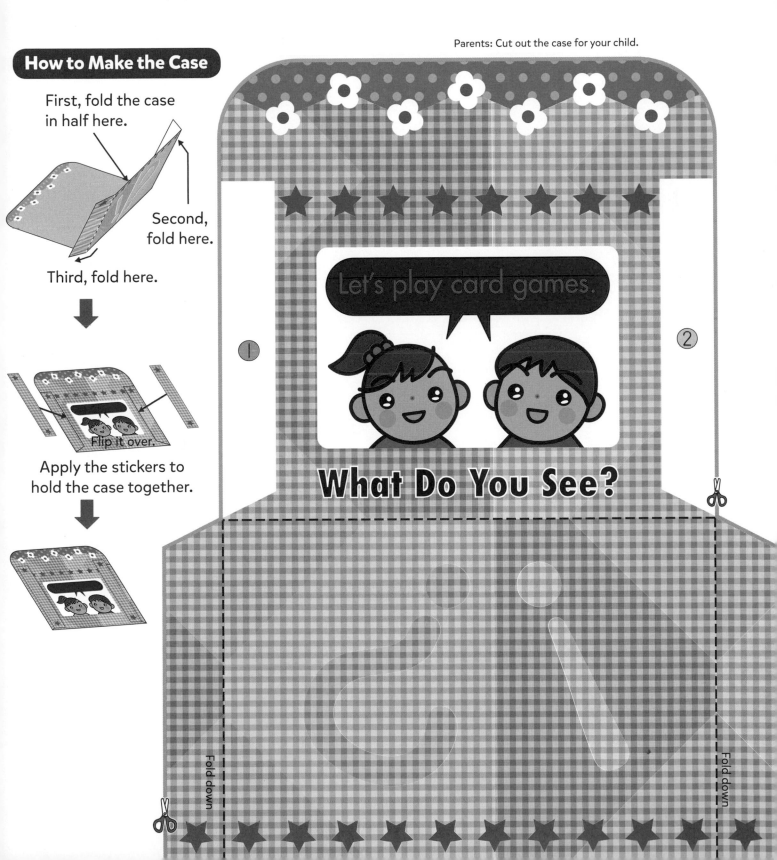

Let's play card games.

What Do You See?

Fold down

Fold down

Let's Play Card Games

To Parents: While playing these card games, your child will practice naming objects and matching spoken language to pictures. For the guessing game, you may have to pull the entire card from the case at first, but your child will gain more confidence as you keep playing. For the naming game, start with three or four cards, and then increase the number of cards.

GOOD JOB!
Sticker

How to Play

Guessing Game
Put all the cards in the case. Slowly pull one card from the case. Players should try to guess what's on the card before it gets all the way out of the case.

What do you see?

A lion

Naming Game
Place the cards on a flat surface. One player names an object on a card. The second player picks the card that was named.

Where is the dolphin?

Make Up Your Own Games!
Extend the fun by asking your child to find all of the veggies or animals. Ask him or her to pick up all of the green or orange objects.

Let's Match the Shapes

To Parents: Cut out the shapes at the bottom of the page and give them to your child to glue in place. Help your child name each shape (triangle, half circle, square) and find its match in the pictures. Ask, "What shape goes here?" as you point to each picture.

GOOD JOB!

Sticker

Glue the matching shapes to the gray area of each picture.

Parents: Cut out the shapes for your child.

Let's Match the Stuffed Animals

To Parents: This activity exercises your child's observational skills. Ask your child to name the types of animals below.

Find the matching pairs of stuffed animals.

Draw a line to connect each matching pair.

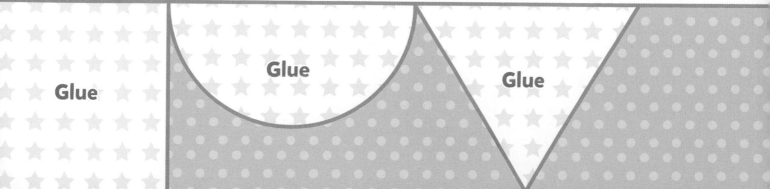

Glue

Glue

Glue

Let's Trace the Number

To Parents: This activity ties the idea of quantity (one) to the symbol that represents that quantity (1) and helps foster proper handwriting.

How many whales are there? Say the number out loud.

Trace the line from 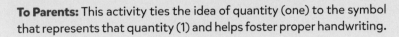 to with your finger. Then, draw it with a crayon.

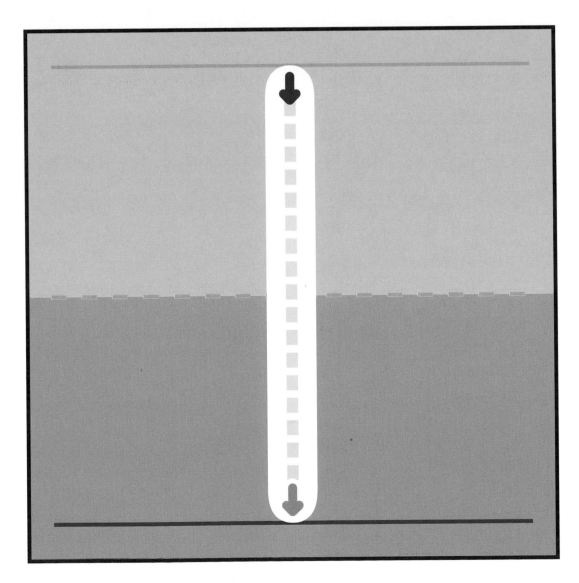

|

44

Let's Trace the Number

To Parents: This activity ties the idea of quantity (two) to the symbol that represents that quantity (2) and helps foster proper handwriting. You may have your child trace the gray dotted line with a crayon if she or he is able.

GOOD JOB!
Sticker

How many birds are there? Say the number out loud.

Then, trace the line from ➡ to ➡ with your finger.

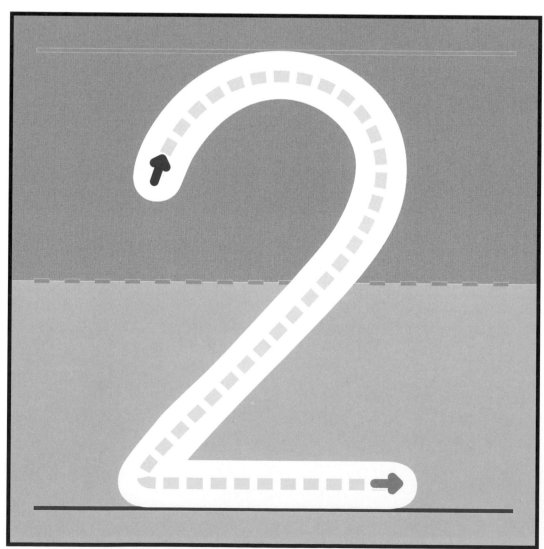

2

Let's Remember the Picture

To Parents: Show the picture to your child for 10 seconds. Then, fold the page and let your child answer a question about what he or she just looked at.

Look at the picture below for 10 seconds. Try to remember as much as you can.

After 10 seconds, fold the page and answer a question.

Fold up

Parents: Cut this line for your child.

How to Play

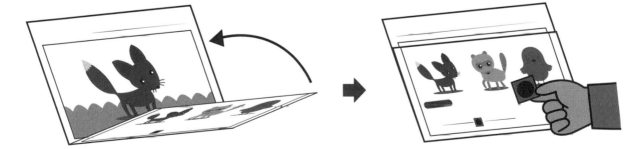

Carefully look at the picture and try to remember. After 10 seconds, fold the page.

Answer the question and apply the sticker.

Let's Find the Difference

To Parents: This activity fosters a child's ability to find differences among a group of objects. In this case, the difference is between a triangle and a square.

GOOD JOB!
Sticker

Find the object that is different. Put the sticker on it.

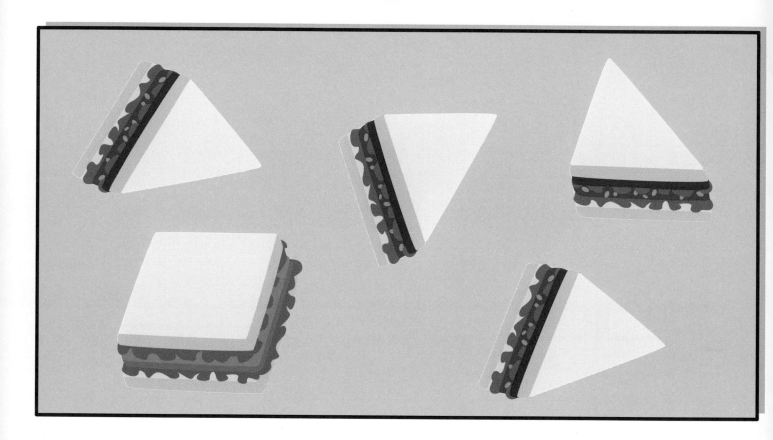

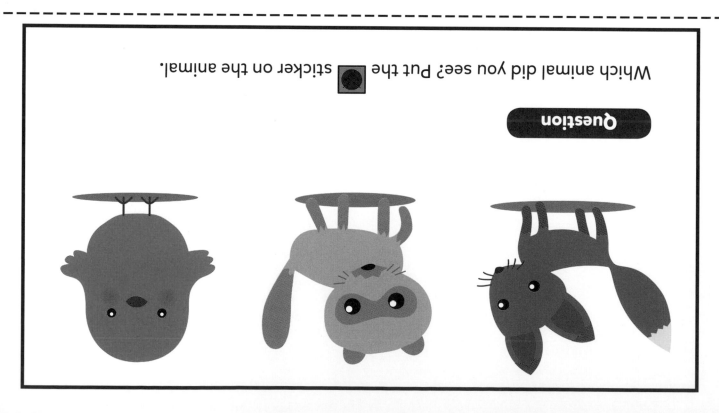

Which animal did you see? Put the ⬛ sticker on the animal.

Question

Let's Find the Matching Trains

To Parents: In this activity, your child will practice matching parts with a whole. Be sure your child starts with the part and then finds the whole by matching the colors and shapes. Repeat this activity so your child learns to spot differences more quickly.

Look at the picture in each ⬜. Which train do the train parts belong to?

Draw a line to connect each match.

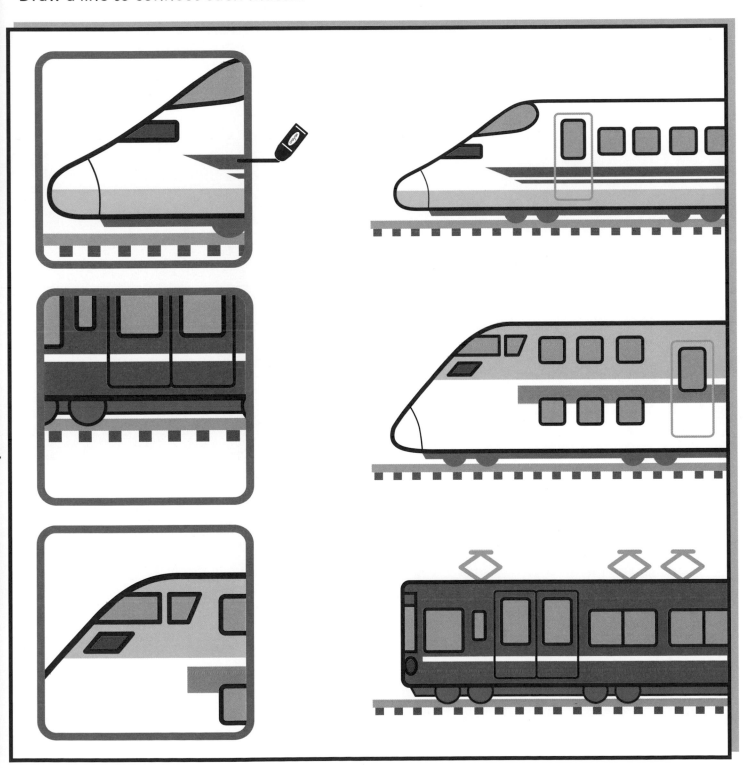

Let's Find the Matching Vehicles

To Parents: This activity fosters the ability to match parts with a whole. Be sure your child starts with the part and then finds the whole by matching the colors and shapes. Repeat this activity so your child learns to spot differences more quickly.

Look at the picture in each ◯. Which vehicle do the parts belong to?

Draw a line to connect each match.

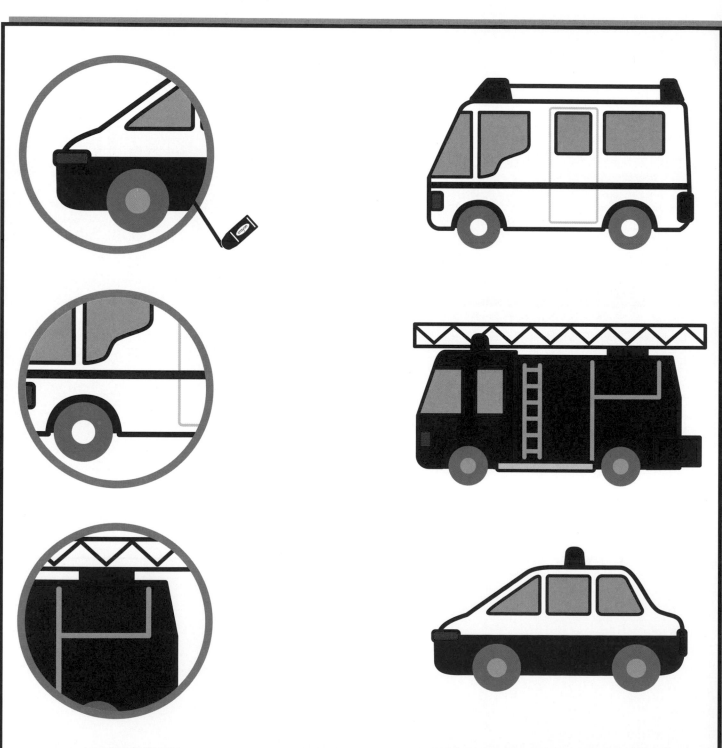

GOOD JOB!
Sticker

Let's Make Lunch

To Parents: Cut out the food rectangles for your child. Tearing, placing, and gluing help develop fine motor skills.

Tear the paper into pieces that look like pieces of vegetables. Mix up the pieces to make a salad. Then, glue the salad to the plate.

How to Play

Tear the food paper into a salad, and then glue it to the plate.

Example

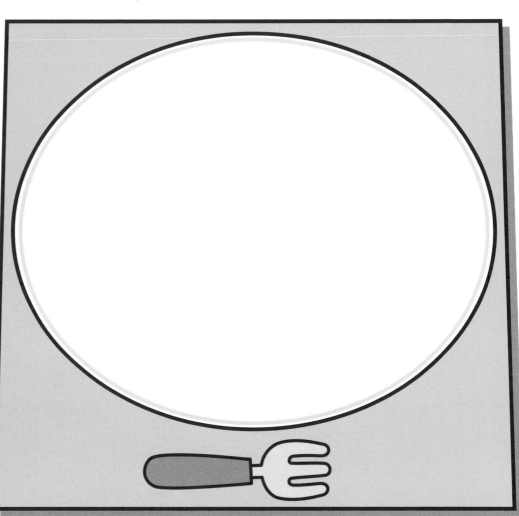

Parents: Cut out the rectangles below for your child.

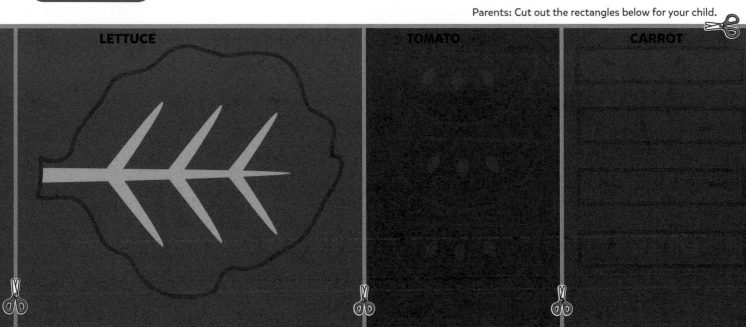

LETTUCE

TOMATO

CARROT

Let's Find the Matching Shape

To Parents: Guide your child to look at the shapes that make up each picture and each shadow.

Look at the picture in the example box. Find the shadow that is the same shape. Put the 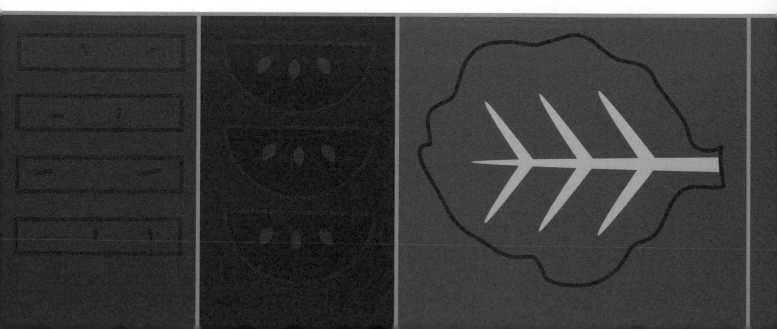 sticker on the matching shadow.

Example

Let's Help Elephant Go to the Bathroom

To Parents: This activity helps to build fine motor skills while creating awareness of potty training.

Put together the toilet. Then, help Elephant go to the bathroom.

How to Make

Glue the lid in place.

Fold

Glue

How to Play

Going potty on the grown-up toilet is fun.

Fold the picture of the elephant. Help Elephant sit on the toilet.

Glue

Parents: Cut out the shapes for your child.

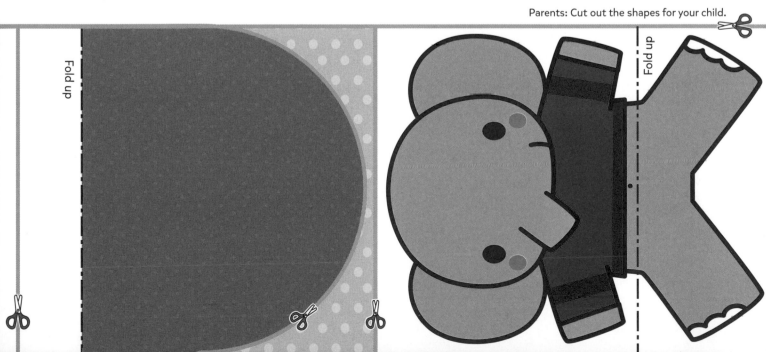

Fold up

Fold up

Fold up

Let's Find the Matching Bread

To Parents: Here, your child will practice matching similar objects within a group. Make sure your child looks at the color and shape of each kind of bread.

Sticker

Look at the bread in the ⬜. Find the bread that matches. Put the ⬤ sticker on it.

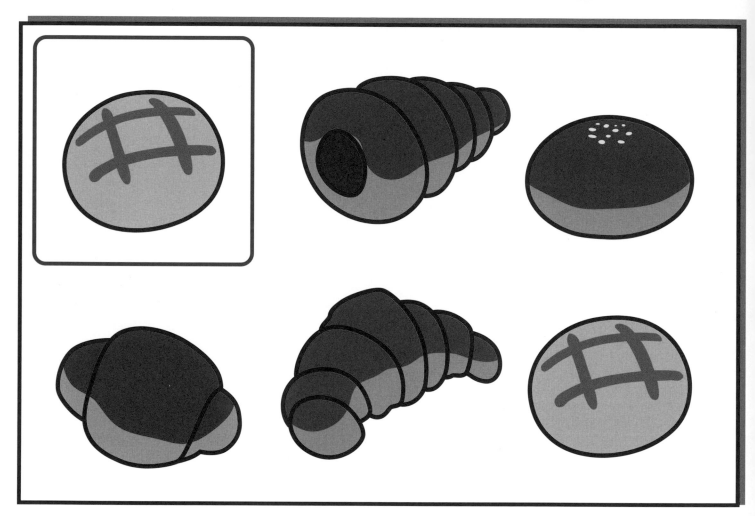

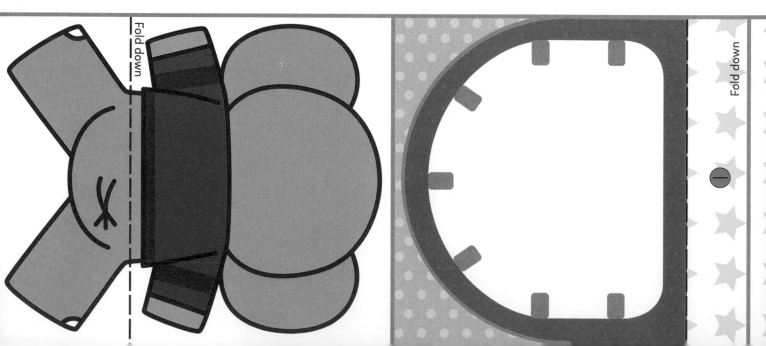

Let's Trace the Letter

To Parents: This activity fosters proper handwriting and language development. Have your child trace the gray dotted line with a crayon if she or he is ready.

Name the animal in the picture. Say it out loud.

Then, trace the line from ➡ to ➡ with your finger.

CAT

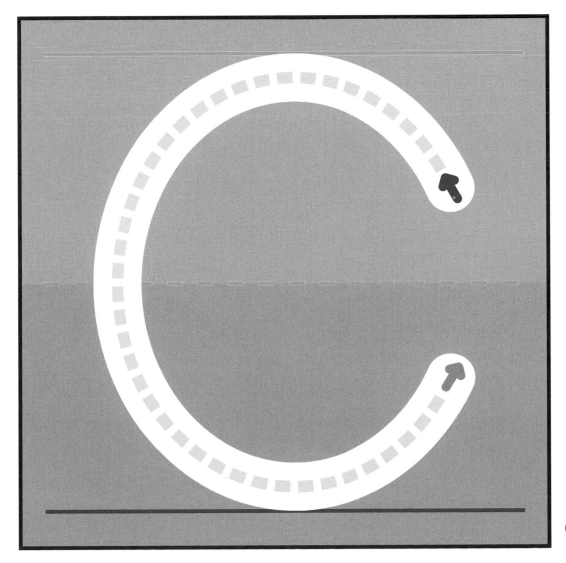

C

Let's Find the Matching Shape

To Parents: Have your child look at the shapes that make up the shadow and the pictures below.

Look at the shadow in the box. Find the picture that is the same shape.

Draw a line to connect the shadow with its matching shape.

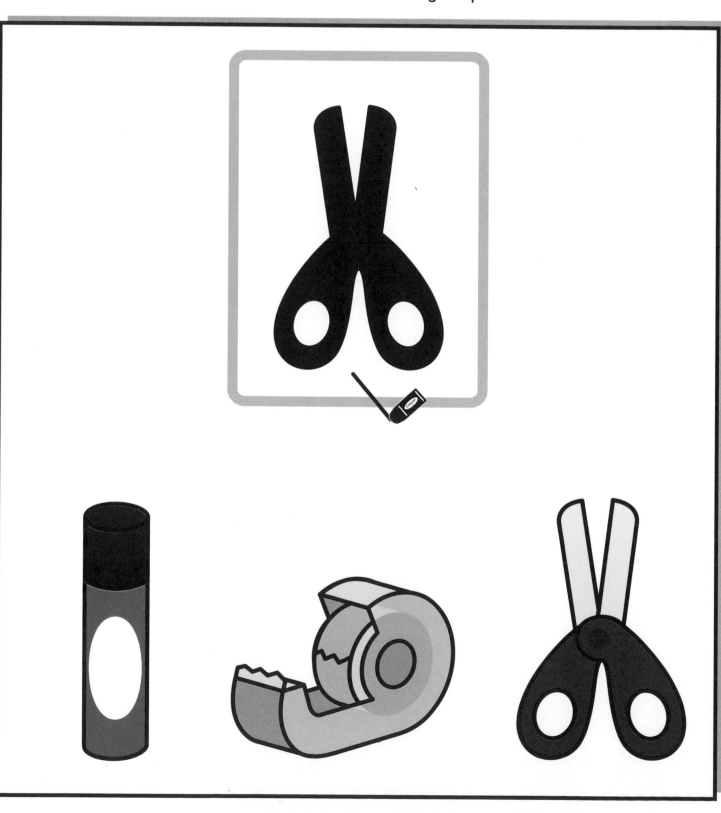

Let's Make Dinner

To Parents: Cut out the food at the bottom of the page and give it to your child to glue in place. Your child can choose to glue the food in any order as long as it fits the box. This activity builds fine motor skills.

Glue the pieces of food to each ⬜ to make a nice dinner.

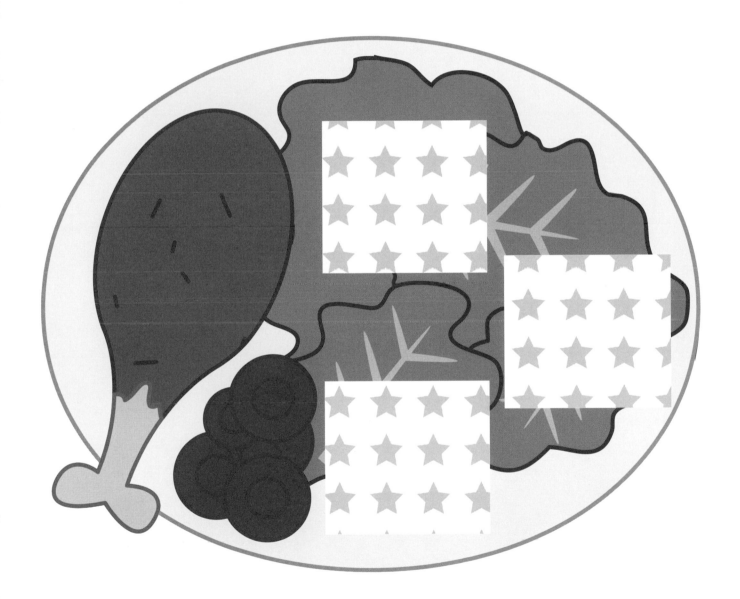

Parents: Cut out the food pieces for your child.

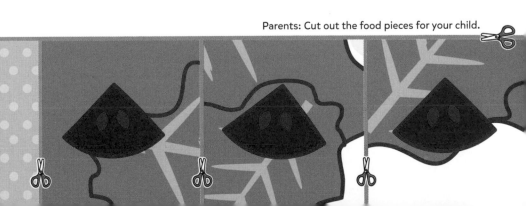

Let's Find the Matching Sweets

To Parents: Guide your child to match three pairs of sweets by looking at shape and color.

Look at the pictures in the box. Then, find their matches on the plate.

Draw a line to connect each match.

Glue   **Glue**   **Glue**

Let's Feed the Hungry Bear

To Parents: This activity builds fine motor skills. Have your child glue both apples inside Bear's mouth.

Feed the apples to Bear. Glue the apples in Bear's mouth.

Parents: Cut out the apples for your child.

Let's Practice Greetings

To Parents: This activity is designed to encourage healthy habits and communication skills. After doing the activity, ask your child what he or she would say just before going to bed at night.

GOOD JOB!

Sticker

What do you say when you wake up? Pretend you just woke up and say it out loud.

Glue   Glue

How to Play

Good morning

Pretend to pull back the blanket. Get your child up to say "Good morning."

Let's Put Fish in the Bowl

To Parents: This activity helps develop fine motor skills while focusing on size relationships. Your child must determine which fish to place on which yellow square, based on its size.

Put the fish in the fishbowl. Glue each of the three fish to the matching ▨.

Parents: Cut out the fish for your child.

Let's Color the Flowers

To Parents: Here, your child will focus on recognizing and naming colors. Ask your child to use crayons to color the flowers. Then ask, "What color are your flowers?"

Color the flowers with any colors you like.

Glue

Glue

Glue

Let's Eat Soup

To Parents: Have your child name each item on the bottom of the page (spoon, pencil, fork) and ask what each is used for. Guide your child to choose the proper utensil for eating soup.

What do you use to eat soup? Put the  sticker on it.

Let's Find the Matching Shape

To Parents: When your child is done, ask how she or he knew which item to pick.

Look at the shadow in the box. Find the picture that matches the shadow.

Draw a line to connect the match.

Example

Let's Find the Matching Items

To Parents: In this activity, your child will work on matching parts with a whole. Be sure your child starts with the part and then finds the whole, by using color and shape. Repeat this activity so your child learns to spot differences more quickly.

Look at the picture in each ◯. Match the parts to the items on the right.

Draw a line to connect the pictures.

Let's Find the Octopus

To Parents: This activity focuses on observation skills. Ask your child if any of the animals in the picture are the same. After your child answers "yes," ask him or her to point to the match. Then, have your child draw a line between them.

Find the same picture as in the box. Then, draw a line to connect the pictures.